# How to Play Tennis

*The Complete Guide to the Rules of Tennis, Tennis Scoring, Tennis Grips and Strokes, and Tennis Tips for Singles & Double*

by Margie Gallagher

# Table of Contents

# Introduction

Tennis is a challenging and fun game, both mentally and physically. It is popular with both women and men, and can be played by small children and retirees alike at varying levels of competitiveness.

If you've just recently begun playing, you may find the sport a bit disorienting, especially when it comes to serving accurately and controlling your shots in general. This book will help you understand the basics of how to play tennis, and it will also help you dial in some crucial yet fundamental tennis skills.

# Chapter 1: Game Essentials

There are *singles* tennis matches—where one contender takes on another individual contender—and *doubles* tennis matches, where two teams of two members each compete against one another. In doubles tennis, if each team is composed of both a male and female player, then it is known as "mixed doubles." Otherwise, it's just called "men's doubles" or "women's doubles."

## *The Anatomy of the Tennis Court*

A tennis court is divided into two sections, your home court and your opponent's court. The net separates your home court from your opponent's court.

Both your home court and your opponent's court contain two 21' x 13.5' *service boxes* near the net. If you are facing the net, the service box on your side of the court on your left-hand side is called the ad court service box, while the service box on your right-hand side is called the deuce court service box. The service boxes are important to the beginning of gameplay. We will talk more about them shortly.

The *baseline* refers to the line at the very bottom (or back) of either end of the court, furthest away from the net. The *baseline*, along with the *sidelines*, which we'll talk about next, define the outer boundaries of the court. In other words, to keep a ball in play, the ball cannot be hit beyond the baseline (deep) nor outside of the sidelines (wide).

The sidelines run along the side of the tennis court, from the baseline to the net. There are actually two sidelines on either side of the court, separated from each other by 4.5 feet. The skinny lane formed between these sidelines is known as the *doubles lane*. The inner sideline is known as the *singles sideline*, which is used during singles competition and defines the boundary of play. The outer sideline defines the boundary of play during doubles competition and is known as the *doubles sideline*.

## Serving and Scoring in Tennis

Understanding how tennis is scored may appear a daunting task to the uninitiated, but it is in fact quite simple. To win a tennis match, you must win a majority of the sets played. Matches are usually played as one set matches, three set matches, and five set matches. Three set matches are most common; unless you just want to play for a shorter time period, in which case you might choose a one set match; or unless you are an advanced male player in a tournament, in which case a five set match may be required. In a one set match, the victor is simply the person or team who wins the set. For a three set match, the victor is the first person or team to win two of the three sets. In a five set match, the victor or victors must win three sets.

Each set is comprised of games; and each game is comprised of points.

To win a set, you must either be the first person to win six games or more, <u>by a margin of no less than two</u>. For example, if Jack and Jill are playing a singles match against each other, and Jack wins six games before Jill wins her fifth game, Jack will win the set. However, if Jill has already won five games by the time Jack wins his sixth, Jack will need to win one more game in order to win the set 7-5 (by a margin of two). If Jill wins again to make the score six games to six, then a tiebreaker must be played to determine the winner of the set. The rules governing tiebreakers will be discussed at the end of this chapter.

*Games* are the fundamental scoring units in tennis. But before we talk about the remarkably odd—yet simple—way in which "games" are scored, we should go over one of the most critical components of tennis, the serve.

At the midpoint of the baseline on either side of the court is a small hash line known as the *centermark*. In both singles and doubles tennis, play is begun when a player *serves* the ball into play. *Serving* involves standing behind the baseline, tossing the ball straight up into the air, and hitting the ball (from a point high over your head) over the net and into the opponent's service box. If the server is standing on the right side of the centermark, then he must serve cross court into the opponent's right-hand service box or deuce court. If he is standing on the left hand side of the centermark, then he must also serve cross court but into the opponent's left-hand service box or ad court. While serving, a player must stand behind the baseline, but may stand anywhere between the *centermark* and the singles sideline. A player must, however, always play the first and every successive odd point in a game by serving rightward of the centermark and into his opponent's deuce court. For the second point in a game and every successive even point, the player must serve leftward of the centermark and into his opponent's Ad Court. The first player or team to serve in a match is determined by coin toss (or more common, a racquet spin) and service rotates with each game played. On each serve, the serving player is given two chances to hit the ball into the appropriate service box; called the "first serve" and if needed, the "second serve." A missed serve—where the player either hits the ball into the net, or somewhere else outside the service box is known as a *fault*. If a player misses his serve twice in a row, it is known as a *double fault*, and the serving player is penalized by losing the point to his opponent. If at any time the serving player serves a ball that touches the net and continues to drop on its first bounce inside his opponent's service court, it is known as a *let*, and the player is allowed to reattempt the serve. So if a player serves a let on his first service attempt, he is given another chance at a first serve. If a player serves the let on his second service attempt, he is given another chance at his second serve.

Points are scored in tennis when a player fails to return the ball to his opponent's legal court, either by hitting the ball into the net or out of bounds or by not hitting the ball at all. Once the ball bounces a second time on either side of the court—in bounds or out of bounds—the point is over and the player who allowed the ball to bounce twice loses the point.

In tennis, whenever a score is given by a judge, player, or spectator, it is proper to state the score of the serving player(s) before stating the score of their opponents.

So if Jack is serving to Jill, and Jack scores the first point, then the score is 15 to love. The odd terms and seemingly random numbers used to score the games in a tennis match may seem strange. Both players begin at "love" or zero. After winning a point, a player moves to "15." After winning another point, the player moves to "30." After winning another, the player moves to "40." So if Jack and Jill are playing a game (Jack is serving) and Jack wins the first point, the score is 15-love. If Jack wins the next point, the score is 30-love. If Jill wins the next point, the score is 30-15. If Jill wins the point after that the score is 30-30 or more commonly called "30 All." In fact, here's how the tie scores are called:

- Tied at 0 points each is called "Love Love"

- Tied at 1 point each is called "Fifteen All"

- Tied at 2 points each is called "Thirty All"

- Tied at 3 points each is called "Deuce"

Similar to sets, games must be won by a margin of two. If the score is 40-love, 40-15, or 40-30, and the serving player (who is at 40), wins the next point, she wins the game. However, if the score of a game reaches 40-40 or *deuce*, then either player must win at least two points consecutively before declaring victory.

Let's walk through a *deuce* scenario with Jack and Jill.

It's deuce (40-40) on Jill's serve. Jill will be serving into Jack's deuce court (as this is the seventh point of the game). Jill wins the point. The score is now *Advantage* Jill. Or Ad Jill, or more commonly called "*Ad In*". Ad In referring to the fact that it is the server holding the advantage rather than the receiver (Ad-Out). If Jill wins the following point she wins the game. If Jack wins the point, then the game is brought back to deuce. In order to win a game that has gone to deuce, a player must win a point on his or her advantage. What this means is that just as in sets, to win, you must defeat your opponent by a margin of at least two points.

To properly state the score of a tennis match, you should include the score of the current game, the number of games won by each of the players in the current set, and the number of sets taken by either player. If Jack and Jill are playing a three set match and they've both won a set a piece and are in the middle of their first game of the third set, then a proper score citation would sound something like: Jack and Jill at a set a piece, and Jack is up 30-15 in the first game of the third set. You'll notice on television, they use a series of columns to notate the score of a tennis match. Each column represents a set and the numbers represent games won. The player with the highest number in any column is the winner of (or is winning) the set which that column represents. On occasion, you will see numbers in superscript which indicate that a tiebreaker was played (or is being played) to determine the winner of the set. The player who scores the most points in the tiebreaker wins both the tiebreaker and the set.

Tiebreakers are played when each player has won 6 games in a set. Unlike normal games, tiebreakers do not use terms like love, fifteen, thirty, forty. They're just scored using normal point names (zero, one, two, three, etc.). To win the tiebreaker, a player must score 7 points <u>and</u> win with a margin of at least 2 points. If Jack leads the tiebreaker 6-5 and wins the next point, he wins the tiebreaker (and thus the set). If Jack and Jill are tied in the tiebreaker at 6-6, either of them can win the tiebreaker (and set) by winning two points in a row. Play continues until one player wins by a margin of at least two.

## Service on tiebreakers accords to the following pattern:

- The player who was due to serve the thirteenth game of the set serves the first point of the tiebreaker (remember, if a tiebreaker is being played, then a game score of 6 to 6 must have been reached during gameplay). This player serves on the rightward side of the center mark into her opponent's deuce court.

- After only the first point is played, service immediately switches to the opposing player who then serves the next two points, first to his opponent's ad court, then his deuce court.

- After the third point is played, the players alternate serves, serving two serves each, and always beginning by serving first to the opponent's ad court, then deuce court.

# Chapter 2: All About The Tennis Serve

## *A Good Serve is a Difference Maker*

Serving in tennis is perhaps the single most relevant difference-making factor in the game. Weaker players with a strong serve have the ability to be competitive even against highly skilled players. If you're looking to be a competitive player, learning to hit a powerful and accurate serve is an essential skill. Unfortunately, like your other tennis skills, a strong serve takes a lot of time and practice to develop. When you first begin playing you probably won't be able to realize much of an advantage between the games where you're serving and the games where you receive. But understanding early on the importance of a good service game can provide you with an important benchmark by which you can measure your progress. As time goes on, you should find yourself winning more often on your serve, than on your opponent's serve.

## *The Service Grip*

To serve well, you should be holding your racquet using the *continental grip*. You can find the continental grip by placing the rim of the racquet head against the court so that the strings of the racquet are at a 90 degree angle from the plane of the court. Now, imagine your racquet is a hammer and you're going to use the rim as the hammer head. Once you find this controlled grip, you're ready to serve. (Another simpler way of finding the continental grip is by imaging you're shaking hands with the racquet).

## The Toss

Any tennis professional knows that a good toss makes all the difference in serving. To toss the ball accurately, hold the ball with your thumb and fingers on either side, as if you were holding a flagpole, or a cup of tea in your left hand. Start with the ball low, near your mid-thigh, bend your knees a bit and use the motion of your body and your arm to toss the ball smoothly up into the air. Ideally, it will float straight up without spinning much. That's not an easy feat, and good players work on this toss regularly to get it this smooth, so don't be disappointed if you find this difficult. And you can certainly still play tennis without a perfect toss.

Let's call the space directly above your head 12 o'clock. You're going to want to toss the ball into the 1'o'clock space, ever slightly ahead of you and towards the net.

There are other serves which require different placements of the ball during the toss, but the 1 o'clock position is the simplest serve to learn.

You're going to want to leverage all of your height on the serve, so toss the ball high enough to make contact at the peak of your racquet's reach, with your arm fully extended and your body fully stretched out. Some professionals advise tossing the ball higher than the peak of your reach and hitting the ball at the peak of your reach as the ball descends. Others suggest that it's best to toss the ball in such a way that it reaches its apex height at the peak of your racquet's reach and is thus perfectly still in the air for a split second and easier to hit. The latter toss strategy will only work if you mobilize your service motion very quickly, meaning that by the time your ball leaves your hand and reaches the peak of your reach, you must be ready to hit it. Some lanky folks may have some trouble with this method. Do some experimentation and find what works best for you.

## The Serve

Remember to keep your eye on the ball after the toss. Fully extend your non-racquet hand or guiding arm up into the air. This will keep your torso upwardly aligned and guide your stroke. Don't drop your arm prematurely. Keep it up for as long as possible, pointing at the ball, until you move to strike the ball with your racquet arm.

Using the continental grip, extend your racquet deep behind your head, as deep as you can go, almost like you're trying to scratch your lower back with it. Keeping your guiding arm in the air and your eye on the ball, time your stroke so that you make contact with the tennis ball at the maximum height of your forward swing.

## Dead Drop Statue Drills

You will have a natural inclination to drop your guide hand (non-racquet hand) too early. Doing this will misalign your torso downward, and you will find you're hitting your serve into the net. Condition your way out of this bad habit by doing simple Dead Drop Statue Drills. With your racquet in hand, throw the ball up in the air, raise your guide hand and hold it there. Let the ball drop all the way to the ground and keep your arm raised at full extension as if you were a statue.

## First and Second Serves

In tennis, the server has two chances to serve accurately (into your opponent's service box). If you miss or fault on the first serve, then you are not penalized a point, but allowed to serve again. If you miss a second time, then you lose the point. These stipulations have a profound effect on the strategy of service.

Most beginner players make the mistake of slamming their first serve as hard as they can, knowing they have a backup chance if they miss. And for all their trouble, they get a first serve accuracy rating (or *first serve percentage*) of 20% or lower. They then follow this up with an extremely light "powder puff" or "tap-in" second serve that does little more than put the ball into play. If you are just beginning, try to slow down your first serve some until you can make it accurate at least 50% of the time. From there, steadily increase the power and make your serve a truly devastating offensive weapon.

## Breaking Serve

When a player loses a game in which he is serving, it's known as a *break*. Breaks are an important strategic element of competitive tennis because they often accompany significant shifts in momentum, as most players have a much better statistical chance of winning the games in which they are serving. When you watch a tennis match where two skilled players are competing, you will often see a back-and-forth exchange of games early on in the match, with each player winning the games where he or she serves the ball (also known as *holding serve*). When one of the players finally breaks his opponent's serve, it is treated as highly significant, because if that player simply holds his own serve for the remainder of the set, then he will win the set.

Many times you will see players who've just had their serve broken rally back hard in the next game in an effort to *break back* and take away their opponent's newly found advantage. Holding one's serve immediately after breaking your opponent's serve is thus known as *consolidating*. Watching professional tennis as a spectator becomes much more interesting once you understand the significance of breaks in service.

# Chapter 3: Grips, Groundstrokes and Volleys

Having a well-rounded command of all the basic tennis strokes will make you a much more difficult player to beat. If you favor your forehand too strongly, as many beginner players tend to do, you will provide your opponent with a weakness to exploit.

## *Forehand Grips and Tips*

The forehand is usually the most comfortable ground stroke for a beginning player. However, as you progress in your game you will find that although your forehand may be your most powerful shot, it is also perhaps the most difficult to control.

The two main power sources behind a forehand stroke is the twisting of the body (hips and shoulders) and the extension of the arm. Always keep your racket back, so you get a full and controlled swing. Begin by rotating your body towards the ball to the point of contact and then move your arm forward through the contact zone.

To add top spin to your forehand stroke, you will need to create upward movement through your stroke. Players have a tendency to create all of this upward movement from the shoulder, but it is important to involve other movement sources as well, beginning with the legs. The legs should

19

begin slightly bent and should extend to initiate the upward motion. A good practice is to isolate the movement in the legs by holding out your racket and using no other movement source but your legs to move your racquet upwards. Do this to get an idea of how much racquet movement you can get out the legs alone.

The other three sources of upward movement are the upper arm (powered by the shoulder), the forearm and the wrist. A good topspin forehand combines all of these movement sources into a smooth, steady and powerful stroke. Don't expect all of this to click overnight. Mastering the top spin forehand and any stroke is going to take practice.

There are three basic grips for the forehand stroke: western, semi-western, and eastern grips. These grips are most easily defined in terms of the placement of one's upper index knuckle on the bevels of the racquet grip. The racquet grip is shaped like an octagon and has eight bevels with "bevel 1" being the top most bevel when the racquet is being held with the strings perpendicular to the ground ie bevel 1 is aligned perfectly with the top rim of the racket.

The *western forehand grip* is good for players who want to play with a lot of power and top spin. Find this grip by placing the palm side of the forefinger knuckle on the fifth bevel (immediately opposite the first bevel). This grip will force a wide and powerful swing with an upturn near the end that will add top spin. One of the drawbacks of this grip is that it is nearly the complete opposite of the continental grip (which you'll use for your serve) in terms of where the hand is placed on the racquet. If you decide to use this grip for your forehands, you will have to practice quickly and accurately switching from one grip to the other.

The *semi-western forehand grip* is a less extreme version of the western forehand grip. Like the western forehand grip, the semi-western grip emphasizes top-spin and coming up from under the ball for the perfect stroke. The semi western forehand grip can be found by placing the palm side of the index knuckle on the fourth bevel of the racket (one bevel counter-clockwise from the bevel used in the western forehand grip).

The safest (though not necessarily most optimal) forehand grip to begin with is the *eastern forehand grip,* which can be found by placing the palm side of the index knuckle on the third bevel of the racket. This grip allows for the flattest stroke, with the racquet strings perpendicular to the ground. Though a flat stroke can cut down on errors, it will be more difficult to generate top spin and play more aggressively with this stroke.

Beginners may find the western and semi-western grips to be a bit awkward at first. It's best to commit to a grip while learning your forehand—even if the grip doesn't feel intuitive at first—and modify and tweak the grip over time as you develop confidence in your stroke and overall game.

## Backhand Grips and Tips

Backhand grips come in two types, one-handed and two-handed. We will use the same numbered bevels to help you find and explore the different backhand grips.

The basic one-handed backhand grip can be found by placing the heel of the racquet hand, along with the palm side of the index knuckle on the first (topmost) bevel of the racquet grip. This backhand grip is also known as the *eastern backhand grip*.

To hit a one-handed backhand, pivot your feet to the left (if you're right-handed) with your right shoulder facing the oncoming ball. Keep your eye on the ball and begin your backswing, turn your shoulders and bring the racket over your chest to prepare for your swing. Don't lower the racket during the backswing. Smoothly swing your racket towards the ball and shift your weight to your front foot. Remain standing sideways as you swing and hit the ball in front of your body. Follow through after hitting the backhand. Keep your elbow straight. The racket stroke should end with the racket facing skyward.

For many players, the two-handed backhand is one of the most controllable shots of the game. Pair it up with a powerful racket and you've got an incredible offensive weapon.

Your grip for the two handed backhand begins with finding the continental grip (described in Chapter 2) for your racquet hand, and then putting your non-dominant hand into place. Do this by taking your left hand (if you are right-handed, and moving your grip down the narrowing throat of the racket until it slides into place on the handle. This is the proper grip for the two-handed backhand.

The two-handed backhand requires a bit of preparation time. As soon as your opponent hits the ball to your backhand side begin positioning yourself roughly in the zone where you'll be making your swing. You will have some latitude for last-second repositioning, but not much. Pivot your feet inward so your front shoulder is square on the ball. Take your racquet backwards over your chest and rotate your shoulders and your hips, keeping shoulders and hips aligned with one another. Swing forward with both hands and try and hit the ball at waist level. Make sure you've got a good foot or so of room in front of you to swing. If the ball is too close to you, then your swing will be cramped. Your right (dominant) hand is going to be supplying most of the power, while your left hand is going to ensure that the shot is controlled. Accelerate through the stroke and shift your weight to your front foot. Be sure to follow through and end with the racquet high as if you're about to come back down for a golf swing.

Putting top-spin on the two handed backhand is definitely possible, just go easy on it, as you will sacrifice a lot of power and it's quite easy to put the ball into the net with too much spin on this stroke.

Another popular backhand shot is the *backhand slice*, which can be used to disrupt an opponent's rhythm during a *baseline rally*—a baseline rally simply refers to a prolonged exchange of shots where both players are playing at or near their own baseline. The backhand slice may also be used to slow down the ball and allow you to recover your position on the court when your opponent is moving you around too much.

To hit a backhand slice, hold your racquet using the continental grip (explained in chapter 2) and use small steps to position your body for the shot. Your right foot (for a right handed player should be in front of your left foot, and you should be positioned in *neutral stance,* meaning that if you were to draw a line between your left and right foot, then it would run parallel to the baseline. Bring your racket backwards across your chest with the racquet head over your shoulder and your elbow bent in a 90 degree angle. Your upper arm should be about parallel with the ground. Swing forward and slightly down. Combine your arm and wrist action to slice at the ball so that the strings of your racket firmly impact the ball. Remember you're slicing the ball, not grazing it. Follow through. At the end of the stroke your racquet will be pointing towards the ground.

### The Volley <u>or</u> How to Turn Yourself into an Impregnable Wall

The *volley* is not really a stroke but a strategic positioning of the racket used to rapidly return an opponent's shot, usually at or close to the net.

The grip used for the volley is the continental grip (see Chapter 2). Usually, when you are using the volley, you are playing close to the net and attempting to return your opponent's shots before they bounce in your court.

To execute a proper volley, start by leaning your bodyweight inward towards your opponent's court. Put your weight on your toes as much as possible. This positioning will allow you a greater degree of agility when you go after your opponent's shot, and you won't lose that potentially crucial half-second of time required to switch your weight off your heels and lunge for the perfect position.

If the ball is approaching your left-hand side, step slightly upwards and inwards with your right foot (for right or left-handed players), over your left foot and let your racquet move with your torso. Make sure your grip is tight and move the racquet downward to make contact with the ball. If the ball is approaching at your right hand side, step slightly upwards and inwards with your left foot, over your right foot, and make contact with the ball using a secure grip and a downward motion. There's a space squarely in front of your dominant shoulder where it's very difficult to field a good volley. Do your best to position your body to avoid this awkward zone.

In the next two chapters we will review some ways in which your serve, volley, and ground strokes can be incorporated into strategic play

# Chapter 4: Game Strategy – Singles

Depending on your strength, speed, and aptitudes, there are a variety of different strategies in singles gameplay that may work best for you. Tennis—singles tennis especially— is a game of positioning. You build offense and control during a point by forcing your opponent into difficult positions and making it hard for him to return your shots with any significant amount of offense, or at all.

A good tennis player sets up a positioning advantage for herself, then concludes by hitting a shot that's unreturnable, also known as a *winner*. If you or your opponent lose a point by mishitting a ball, so that it goes deep, wide, or in the net, it's known as an *unforced error*. You will suffer through a lot of these as a tennis beginner. Don't get discouraged.

## *Serve and Volley*

If you are able to develop a strong serve—meaning that your first serve lands accurately over 50% of the time and is not easily returned by your opponent—then a *serve and volley* strategy may be your best bet.

The serve and volley strategy involves hitting a hard serve to start and quickly switching your grip to the continental and approaching the net. The objective is to use your serve to force your opponent into hitting a weak return that you can play at the net.

In general, playing a ball at the net gives you much better shot at hitting a winner. The trick is forcing your opponent into a slow, weak shot that you can approach and drive home.

### Baseline Rally

Players with excellent groundstrokes and less than stellar serves may prefer playing near the baseline and staying away from the net. Though it's harder to hit a winner from the baseline, it's a lot easier to cover the court and defend while playing from this area.

A popular way to play from the baseline is to continually try and push your opponent backwards by trying to hit deep balls that bounce just inside your opponent's baseline.

Baseline Rally players must also be aware of *no man's land,* referring to the court space beginning about two feet inside the baseline and ending just inside the service boxes on your side of the court. If you get stuck in this area, perhaps by returning a short ball or backing off of net play, then a deep hard passing shot will be nearly impossible to return. Give yourself a fighting chance and stay out of no man's land.

### The Mad Spinster

You'll run into some players who play at the club level who like to put spin on <u>everything</u>. If you have enough tricks up your sleeve – top spin, side spin, spin on the serve etc. – this strategy can disorient opponents and make them more likely to error.

Also, putting spin on the ball can force your opponent to adjust mid-shot and give up some control over ball placement. If your opponent is going through a major positioning adjustment because of your ball spin, consider going to the net and looking for a weak shot to play.

## *The Mental Game*

One of the most important things to realize while playing competitive tennis, especially in singles play, is that tennis is just as much a mental game as it is a physical game, if not more so. Players with less skill and less experience beat superior players all the time because the superior player loses focus mentally. This may be perhaps true in most any sport, but the mental dynamics of tennis are unparalleled. There's a reason why players on the ATP and WTA freak out when there's too much noise during their serve, or when the judge allows their opponent too much time to prepare and rest in between points. Focus and momentum are precious commodities during a tennis match.

If you find yourself becoming mentally psyched out, or starting to get nervous or choking, there are two recommendations I have.

- **Trick #1:** Stop thinking about how you're playing. In fact, stop thinking about the game at all. Start thinking about what you're going to eat for dinner, what movie trailer you saw on TV recently that looks good enough for a trip to the box office. Try to remember specifically which pair of underwear you're wearing (without cheating by sneaking a peak). Try to multiply the number 283 times 4791 in your head. Think about anything *except* the game you're playing.

- **Trick #2:** Chew a piece of gum. This jaw-smacking motion has the ability to give you a sense of calmness and casualness... When you're chewing gum, how seriously can you really take yourself? How bad or critical can any situation be? See, when you're chewing gum, you'll naturally become more laid back. Chillin', gum-smackin', easy-going, Joe Cool, straight from the hammock between two palm trees on the beach.

While both of these "tricks" seem a bit crazy, they really do address the heart of what's most likely happening when you become nervous or start choking. Most likely, you're "in your head" too much, and over-analyzing the mistakes you're making. Problem is, with tennis, sometimes it's easier to correct a technical error by going back to subconscious muscle memory, rather than trying to "think" yourself back to the proper grip or form. By taking your mind out of the negative or overly-critical realm, you're allowing your body the opportunity to find its natural muscle memory again without your brain getting in its way.

# Chapter 5: Game Strategy – Doubles

Doubles tennis in today's culture tends to be a little less intense and a little more social. Tennis clubs will often favor doubles play, as it both accommodates large memberships when court space is limited while also instigating socialization among club members. Nevertheless, the strategy that goes into doubles play should not be ignored. Here's a rundown:

## *One Up, One Back*

The most common way to play doubles is for one team member to play the net while his counterpart plays at the baseline. This strategy gives the team a chance to make winning net shots, without sacrificing court coverage.

While utilizing this strategy, it's important that the team members retain a degree of accountability for their respective sides of the court. The net player must always guard the doubles lane on his side of the court to prevent unreturnable passing shots down the lane.

## Two Up

Playing two players at the net is both risky for your team and intimidating for your opponents. While it's significantly more difficult to hit a passing shot when two players are guarding the net, a nicely hit lob shot with a lot of top spin will be virtually unreturnable.

## Two Back

As in singles play, concentrating your resources on the baseline is a more conservative approach to strategy. Playing two back will maximize court coverage but will give you fewer opportunities to bedazzle your opponents and any spectators with scintillating winners.

# Conclusion

The more you play, watch and study tennis, the more you will enjoy it. If you are looking to improve your skill level, try and play against a variety of opponents and try to find people to play with who are either at your skill level or slightly better.

It's also a good idea to invest in a higher quality racquet, especially once you are able to hit hard shots with a decent degree of control. Some sports or hobby shops will let you sample or rent racquets for a few days for a marginal cost. The term you should use when asking, is "I'd like to *demo* a racquet." In some cases, the shop will allow you to use your rental fees as credits towards the purchase of the racquet you eventually choose to buy.

The best, most expedient way to find good tennis partners is to join a club. There are a variety of tennis clubs available at prices ranging from free to very expensive. Check online or at your local recreation center. You can also search for "tennis" at MeetUp.Com. Likewise, you can always consider joining a USTA sanctioned club or flex-league if your work schedule is challenging.

In any case, know going into it that there will be a learning curve, and in order to really enjoy tennis, you'll have to get better at it. But to get better at it, you'll need to go through a rough patch first. Getting your mind wrapped around that will make you a lot less likely to quit just because you're not a great player right away. Adopt a positive attitude, and tell yourself you're just going to enjoy a day outside, running around, getting some exercise. If you can do that a few days a week, then you'll end up a pretty decent player in a matter of about 3-6 months. And at that point, the fun of the game becomes limitless.

Finally, I'd like to thank you for purchasing this book! If you enjoyed it or found it helpful, I'd greatly appreciate it if you'd take a moment to leave a review on Amazon. Thank you!

Made in the USA
Lexington, KY
30 June 2016